AF231180

You May Applaud Now

Elizabeth P Brooks

Sula Too Publishing Tampa Florida

Dedication

for my children Max and Quint.

May you always GROW IN FAITH,
embrace HOPE
be filled with LOVE for humanity
ENJOY the JOY of the Lord
Knowing there would be no PEACE
without FORGIVENESS.

Acknowledgements

A toast and heartfelt gratitude to my parents Robert and Gerardina Brooks who are always alive in my heart. Fond memories of Excelsior Printery Fyzabad, Trinidad. Pure love and affection to Marcano Race.

Blessings Galore to my *Beautiful* sisters in Christ at Grace Family Church Women's Ministry Ybor City.

Enormous gratitude to Janine Pickett, Indiana Voice Journal(IVJ), an online publication, where versions of my poems appeared. *You May Applaud Now* May 2015, *Indescribable Pleasure*, August Nature Issue; *Full Circle and Somehow Encountering God's Presence* –Grace issue Nov/Dec. Also truly grateful for being awarded a column in her second online journal, *Spirit Fire*.

February 2016 IVJ issue #18 *Look at Me and IVJ* special *Ekphrastic edition issue #19, Broken and Hunted, and Unbridled Potential. That Little Girl and Your Sound Your Style* will appear in IVJ March themed issue on Music.

Pastor Dwane, thank you for introducing my poem, Full Circle to the ladies. Thank you Lady Indera, Lady Marie, Pearlette, Shonnette, and Erica.

Author's Note

This is my season!

The time is now and the place is at the heart of my community - human dignity.

Poetry has allowed me to connect the dots. It creates a place for my heart to bleed, to heal, to love, to reveal to pour into another and to celebrate life while pleading for peace, truth and justice for all humanity.

Thank you, Dr. Martin Luther King, Jr. for your love, your wisdom, your commitment and most of all your sacrifice.

Proverbs 29:7
"The righteous considereth the cause of the poor: but the wicked regardeth not to know." KJV

It is a delight and a privilege for me to Step UP to have my say... because I'm tired of the discontent! Can we have a change of heart for humanity?

Proverbs 15:3-4 suggests The Soft Answer
"A wholesome tongue is the tree of life but perverseness is a breach of the Spirit" KJV

To the Christians, where is Christ in all of this? I am talking to all of them that I offend.

How corrupt and warped can a human mind be to concoct such a concept of inferiority and cause massive destruction, world chaos, grief and pain to humanity? How corrupted, distorted and twisted?

Can one ever cease to perpetuate a lie? Insanity can believe its lie which is beyond ugly, sad and frightening.

How can the oppressors walk and lift their heads? They think they are wealthy, respectable and free but the color of their souls must be Black like me.

When they are thinking and listening who is their voice within?

Injustice can only prevail when there is a common thread which creates a fabric woven with greed, deceit, immorality and without dignity and responsibility.

Too little is being done and too much is left unsaid and too many people are silent, indifferent and choose to be ignorant.
But we can find abundant joy by loving humanity, celebrating each other and living with integrity and dignity.

One of the members of my tribe invited me to make a pact with her to change the world.

Join us! Let us change the world NOW!

Contents

You May Applaud Now!

We are BEAUTIFUL
We are pumps, lace, silk and satin
long skirts, boots, short skirts,
sequins, pearls, leather,
leggings and jeggings

We are educators, doctors, writers and
lawyers, pantsuits, power dress,
diamonds, bangles and rings

We are astronauts, actors, artists, students and
athletes, nurses and care-givers.
We are Nobel prize winners in every category,
in literature and peace, chemistry and
physics, medicine and economics

Because we are believers, givers, fighters and protectors.
We are mothers, friends, lovers, pastors, politicians and wives
We are royalty, CEO's and CFO's
Yes, we are in the boardroom and
a force to be reckoned with

We are resilient, perceptive and wise,
your sixth sense,
your conscience
your universe

We are the lighter side of you,
we are the depths you want to conquer
we are gentle, passionate, kind, beguiling, saucy and sassy
we are Mother Earth and Mother Nature naturally,
we give birth

We are the progenitor of ideas at times
we are not what you see but
we are what you get.

A lot of trappings
sometimes too much baggage or
over-stuffed carryon luggage

We can be your worst nightmare –historically,
a hurricane or your most vivid delightful dream
which takes you through the bliss of death and dying
reverberating - weeping and
we bring you back again - spent,
but full of joy and sometimes laughter
you are given a second wind
you can breathe again – to dream again

Oh! We are very worthy of your praise and
we are everywhere,
but you are a part of us and we, you.

We are BEAUTIFUL!

And we will not be abused nor be denied
you are no better than us nor we any less than you

Yet by His Grace, we birthed you
you are the gift,
now it is time for us to nurture you and
we are well-quipped
because we are
bold, fearless and God-Inspired women.

We are Beautiful!
I'll take my bow!

Agony and Irony

Every day I give praise and thanks
to my Holy Father and
promise to do His will with trust and faith
I am assured of His love
knowing He will protect and provide for me, always.

Then with a twist I look in the mirror.

Who am I?
I see shades of doubts
subtle callousness, emptiness

I try to hide my fears and secrets
I strip my skin with bleaching cleansers
use renewing masks, eye cream and concealer
to cover my painful scars and ugly blemish
so one cannot discern my tormented nights and
bleary eyes as well as
not feeling well behind my distressed smiles

Who am I?

It is not just superficial
it is also complex, internal, several layers deep within,
more secrets haunt me
reminding me of reality
which really does not comfort me

My heart beats at a frenzied pace and
my boiling belly aches
as the evil one taunts and reminds me that
I am nothing - nobody.

Who am I?

I use foundation garments
to cover flubs flabs and bulging gut
even when wearing denim or linen
few people can figure me out

It is a bit difficult
because they cover too and
don't know who they really are

Together we cover fears, pride and self-hate
then we overdo and get in a rut

Father it does not matter to You
if we are in disguise.
To You we are naked, all exposed
You see it all.

We cannot hide our flaws
not the ugliness, self- hate, sin or pain.
Thank You, Father for loving us
You see also our sweetness and overwhelming goodness
that will not diminish
but will flourish with our faith like a mustard seed,
from the fruit of the spirit
regardless of my human error
sometimes I get a glimpse of me,
who and whose I am
yet I continue to act so foolishly.

Such agony and irony
I cannot hide my identity.
Father forgive me,
Stay with me Lord!

Broken and Hunted

Things are tough and times are rough.
You feel broken and hunted
vulnerable and threatened.

You are not an endangered species or
on any protected list
because you are not wild or an animal

Stay alert to disruptions and
doubts and squabbles flashing lights and sirens,
all oppression- subtle and blatant

That is not news but has always been the norm.
Don't let that get you down or invade your spirit.
Continue to stay in tune to hear and
develop what is your spirit,
to discern the magic and the joy within,
that no one can take away from you.

Comply to protect your body.
Don't be defiant!
Set yourself apart
Be true to your spirit
You have work to do.
You are authentic.
Continue to dream!

Live the life you imagined.
You are a wonderful human being
who will contribute to the heart of your community.

Unbridled Potential

A remarkable opportunity
which reveals beauty and strength.
Unbridled potential, reflected from within little ole me
manifested as distinctive and exotic steadfast and mysterious.

Focused in solitude perked ear listening to that small voice,
eye showing determination full of intent,
as I experience being in the Presence.

Image defined. On water as natural as solid ground.
I feel the power and magnitude
of the burning sensation of my passion,
the boldness of my vision
which is sometimes threatened,
sometimes elusive when confronted
with challenges, with tension, as I transition

Because others are not able to see
what has been revealed to me
the brilliance of my talent
the beauty of my gift
that the world eagerly awaits

I am very blessed, encouraged and fortunate
that my purpose has been made clear to me
and I know what I am entrusted to do.
I have the choice to recede or blend in.

But for now my audience is quite selective.
It is an audience of one, my protector, provider, and life-giver.
He is counting on me to utilize my full potential
to use the gifts He has given me.
I have been chosen
I am Spirit led and Spirit fed filled with divine inspiration.

Stirring My Hub Up

I'm tired of the vitriol,
I'm tired of the denunciations of my character.
Slowly dripping with venom
from ferocious yet invisible fangs.

This is socially complex,
you don't have the capacity to understand.
Please examine your perspective
so you can discuss and engage it
because you always exude it.

I experience it every day
from you at work and at play
what's lacking is compassion
only then you will see the truth
of the social dynamic between you and me.

You are dismissive.
You would not look at my character
to gain the value of diversity to see the similarity.
You cheat yourself, me.
You cheat the world, your children… you cheat everybody.

Shame and Disgrace

Any ordinary dictionary will state
Inhumane, means lacking the qualities of a human being,
but my faith holds strong for all of humanity.
Though some are hateful and petty and
oppose goodwill to all men.

What is their contribution to humanity?
What can they espouse
that would be uplifting, illuminating?

Instead of shamefully spewing obstructionism
and McConnelism, that is so very offensive to humanity.

I am left with a variety of questions.
Why don't the cronies feel
 Violated? Disgraced?

When will we have unity?
Humanity is the ability to love all of mankind.

Humanities,
to enrich the Spirit of man.
Are they as confused as I am
by the three-fifths compromise
clause in the constitution?

Discovery

We are in a crisis with our identity.
We reside in a hopeless state
born and bred in a dreamless state
so distant from another reality
Our despair cannot be contained in our mind-set.
Let's breakthrough our limited skills set.

Now dear God, give us dreams and hope
teach us how to claw, scratch and fight
not watch TV all day and every night.

We must be inspired to think critically,
But some of us are entertained
by giving the cable company money. Really?

To watch someone else fulfill their dream.
You must adjust your mental antenna
Something is fundamentally wrong with that picture.

Evolve from the muck and mire.
Shonda is the message not just the messenger,
who uses her imagination and determination.
Show her your appreciation by imitation.
Her dream should be the match to ignite
your fire.

This is your Life.
You are a participant.
You must participate in your development.
What's your dream? What's your legacy?
What is the how's and the why's basic questions
in philosophy begin with an evaluation

Where am I? and Where am I going?
Have high expectation
hope, dream, set goals
Write it out. Get up!
That's the first step

Look up, be in awe of His majesty
life goes on, jump up, press on,
you can win, if you fail, that's ok- try again,
choke out hopelessness.
Define yourselves, yes stake your claim,
you can dig a little deeper, don't stop.
You are about to hit the jackpot.

Hope is the breeding ground for dignity
Look at the acorn and the oak tree.
There is always a journey and a destination.
Every path, road and every trail
has bends and turns, sand and stones
Who am I? What and why?

Enough of those sleepless nights worry days and
don't care-that you don't care ways
Cast off doubt, dust and chains you have heart.
Share your vibe, your energy and remember
we are the economic pulse of this country.

So flex some muscles, release the chains,
mentally hulk it out, infuse your brains
with selective thought and deliberate action.
That will ignite your passion and yield your purpose.
Maintain your new rhythm,
remain laser focused.
You have the capacity.

You are blessed with the authority and
the responsibility, to experience your sacred fire and
breakthrough to freedom.
As you reposition yourself
you will not be defeated!

You may stumble and fall
but you will rise up.
You will forever stand tall.

Somehow

It was not war
that allowed me to discover
that life is filled
with enormous blessings and opportunities

It was not a riot
that inspired me to search beyond
my fears and inadequacies

It was not rage
that fanned the burning flame inside of me
to insist on love and absolute beauty

Somehow
It was -You
You became
the source of my power

It was You
who ignited my hunger.

Look at Me

When I awake at the break of day
and I listen to the highlights of overnight
I'm quickly reminded of how much you struggle
with my blackness

Another brutal incident
an indictment of ugliness, pain,
grief, sin and shame.

And I endure your criticisms,
all of your attitude your low expectations, your indifference but
you too, are a victim of the establishment
yet you continue very subtly to oppress me
with built in systems that sanitize and legalize the perpetrations.
I am constantly sideswiped and you are oblivious.

Bewildered then, I look at my reflection in the mirror,
and I see what God my heavenly Father sees in me.
So I boldly accentuate my looks, full lips,
my natural hair, braids, dreadlocks or nappy
for variety and flavor
I add extensions or color which does not define me,
look at me.
Deep down, I'm very clear about my character.
But I'm forced though blessed to turn to my hub,
my spiritual mentors in my community.

We have to consciously strategize how to promote ourselves,
 how to protect ourselves, our children who we are.

You must engage in dialogue with me
that's enlightening and nurturing to both sides.
You cannot continue to walk around
uninformed and with blinders on.

There is value in diversity but
you must have knowledge and sensitivity
What's clearly lacking is empathy.
Look! Look, Look at me,
at minorities collectively.
To some we maybe a succulent thing
others sweet and sour, to more still,
a bit too tart.

Look at me.
But you must have insight to look deep
within below the surface of the melanin
of my beautiful skin.

It's not just cafe-latte, espresso, cocoa-tea,
molasses, cinnamon or brown sugar.
You are unable to recognize,
this is where my faithful spirit, and
my humanity is housed and flows throughout.

I'm confident because it washes and it cleanses me.
That's why I am the epitome of beauty.
I stand on faith to duplicate
with knowledge and certainty, my vision
 my wisdom, my outward look,
my inner beauty which is radiant with Abundant Joy
and that - is my victory.

Look at me.
My enduring faith,
my gratitude, my dignity and yes, my humility.
These are the attributes that enhance my beauty.

I know who I am,
I know whose I am
I am more than you think I am.

Your Sound, Your Style

I hear the music in the street,
sweet guitar strings,
your sound, your style,
the applause of thunder and
a New York summer storm.
Your music stirs my soul.

Then the recognition in your eyes as
you spot me weaving through the crowd
amidst the faint sweetness of angelic faces and
scoops and tons of people at crosswalks
on the streets coming from art museums/ of pumping hearts
focused, some laser focused, on a subway ride like zombies,
but your music interrupts their stride.
Some linger others stop to hear you play for awhile.

After being with my friends, in the heat
shopping to the beat of the street fairs and
the experience of bundles of fun.

You and I return home to a light supper,
share a glass of wine.
Then twin showers and giggles,
a body massage from those
hands, melting in your arms like clockwork,
then I fall asleep with a painted smile
to the soft jazzy lullaby
of your voice and your sweet strum of the guitar.

Full Circle

Father God, nothing is hidden from You! You know my brokenness,
my pain and my foolishness.
Still You have blessed me with beautiful gifts.
I was a child wrapped up in a whirlwind, ventured into the unknown,
outmatched, outsmarted, outwitted.

Now, adorned with ex- husbands and enough lovers, tossed aside
to recognize, the archer was an impostor. He had a deceitful bow, he
couldn't shoot an arrow.
I know now that wasn't Cupid - then -
It had to be me, Marvin Gaye's music in me
in my head, groovin' to "Sexual Healing."
And David Rudder's soca
praising me as a Bacchanal lady
And Bob Marley's No Woman No Cry

Marvin, Rudder, And Marley
you promised carnal pleasure,
but it was all unquenched fire,
what's left is the remnant of a bitter root embedded within.
Unaware of the truth, in search of intimacy,
I felt my passion build then wane again, unfulfilled.
Dissatisfied, bored disillusioned!
For me real love was elusive,
nothing is guaranteed but
I have a surging need

A joyful heart and a joyous spirit.
It is my ground of being, where I come from;
a place which glows and blooms;
where an eagle can renew its wings,
so I pressed on;
hungering for something different, hoping,
constantly growing, stretching forward –searching.

And He waited.
Arms outstretched.
He knew I would come.
I'm embraced, redeemed not condemned.
Drenched in true love,
now my thirst is finally quenched
by my master, the fountain of the living waters.

I'm the woman at Jacob's well.
I am overwhelmed.
I always wanted to be the way
He designed me.
To be free,
Thank you Lord!
Oh Jesus!

My Lord and my King.

Long Stem Glasses

Long stem glasses sexy and appealing
I fell into the trap of glamorizing.

At night I enjoyed my long stem glass
with robust red wine
had a drink or two now that the object has been defined
I broke the hook that got me.

No, not my long stem glass
it's the drink
that almost grabbed me
believing I needed one every night
but my glass can still seduce me.

Now I enjoy water, juice or unsweetened tea
in my goblet,
alcohol I choose not to have it
not any day, night or
celebration.

My mind feels free
my body much better and healthier
talked to a few of my peeps
who agreed with me
their minds and their
bodies now too are free.

I See You

You are not invisible
don't cower or walk in anyone's shadow

Stand UP

You are covered
by the shadow of His wings.

Wake UP

the heart of the wise, poor and good
knows both sadness and gladness.

What is done is done and
cannot be undone
but the living can become alive and strive
what appears abase
will abound with dignity and grace.

Step UP!

1989 Part l

Something is definitely wrong with this man
I tried to see how badly he was hurt
I needed a game plan.
Enlisting others in the street was like
pulling wisdom teeth but
something is definitely wrong with this man.

He was not bleeding
and yes, he was conscious
but there he was lying on the sidewalk
we can't leave him lying here,
I shouted something is definitely wrong with this man.

Passers-by looked at me incredulously with transparency
I realized this man had become part of the landscape
and I am in a foreign land they glared at me
something is wrong with this woman.

I wanted to scream
wake up from this nightmare but
instead bowed my head, and stooped, eyes full of tears

He watched me, still lying there
he said "I'm ok, I'm ok"
I walked away and became a New Yorker that day

That memory still haunts me today
I walked away broken hearted, broken spirited, inept,
because I did not say,
here take my hand Get Up!

1989 Part II

Riding the subway
a man without a home
stretched out his hand opened palm
I placed a dollar in it knowing for him that was not enough
but I felt generous

During the ride
another outstretched hand, another opened palm
another dollar given, then two and three
with empathy I looked around and
recognized another heart-wrenching norm.

Look Ahead

Like a healthy plant

With growing roots
Grounded and vertical
Taking its nutrients From the soil
Basking in the sunlight
Delightful in our environment
Swaying in the breeze
Replenishing our seed

Aware of our purpose
To make our presence felt
And grace our landscape

As we blossom in full bloom
Providing food and shelter
in all the glory for the public good.

That Little Girl

She ran everywhere she went she was so shy,
hid behind her mother's skirt, she was so shy,
she would pluck her eyelashes out when people talked about how
thick they were.
She could not stand to hear
how little she was, had pretty hair she was so shy.

Everyday her mother stuck her head out the door
"don't run." But off she went out of breath.
She ran all the way, some said
"'she'll definitely be late for school today, poor thing!"
But she was fast - so swift and on time, almost late -
close call but she did her morning ritual
danced for her Mommy and Daddy.
Her parents watched as music took her into another dimension.

When her Daddy worked the morning shift
she could not dance for him
but her Mommy was always there,
she danced for her to her surprise -
she sometimes looked up, there was her Daddy, "
my relief came early today," he would say, so happy
but so spoiled she would pout and frown in obvious glee,
then smile and dance, and dance and dance
then run, and run, and run again to school that day.

That little girl, shy on the outside but
she had an internal drive always glowing,
brave and bold on the inside.

When she danced she was mad with ecstasy
her body was ripe with rhythm
you could see the soul of that little girl
who still moves with rhythm to the beat of every sound.

The Power of Oral Tradition

A one word identifier
kept my maternal line together
origin, location, as
He looked upon water, water
no name but it doesn't matter
a name is a what like a title
to a thing that can be
changed by choice as in marriage.

This poem is about the power
of a who, the spirit of who
which flows like a healing river
no label tossed at you but
with foresight and insight
my ancestor cleverly
demonstrated the dynamic
power of oral tradition
the Spirit of oral tradition.

We were all mesmerized by Haley's saga and
through Kunta Kinte's eyes
But, my family knew another man's
courage and spiritual fortitude
of being African,
an indignant warrior!

We celebrated him who knew
he was stolen, kidnapped
but he didn't share his name
he shared from where
he was stolen.
Every time he opened his mouth
he uttered "Yoruba Yoruba!"
looking for another

searching' knowing there is
strength in numbers and the value of
communication to fight to rebel
he knew his name would be changed
but nothing or anyone could replace

the Yoruba spirit.

Long before computer technology

and DNA tests
my family was already defined.
For generations many children
would repeat and say as they play
we don't know the African man's name
but, he was Yoruba, Yoruba!

A man without a name left us
a great legacy. That capacity
for insight gave my family
the spirit of resiliency.
We know who we are
WE are warrior people!

Yoruba! Yoruba!

Royal Blood

Adorned in purple velvet robed in royalty,
sensual silk threads, fragile flowing with
freedom of movement below the crown of her head
to the tip of her feet.

A natural encounter with cotton fibers woven with passion
blended in a sea of pink satin expressed in a rebellious fashion.

Now, a creation of bold graphic designs
in colored patterns and jeweled tones and
morphed into a panorama of texture -
beautiful fabric speckled with untold secrets
of forbidden love my family dynamic - unchanged –
still royal blood!

The Lure of the Moon

I was awakened to the presence of
moonbeams on my bed,
splashed across my pillow, my face.

It's almost 3:00 AM.
Sleep has lost the battle - will no longer come
the middle of my night.
Awestruck by my new visitor.
He's stunning.
The pull of sleep,
the lure of romance,
I cannot look away.
I tiptoe to my window,
to bed and back again.
I want more of this private, gentle,
nurturing holy time.

Very early last night, I glanced at him
through the blinds of my living room
on the other side.
I even peeked at him from my guest room -
each time I blew him several kisses.
He flooded my house with his reflection -
from the east side.
I thought this could be a wild night.
I resisted going to bed, but he knows
where to find me.

We were together,
fully aroused,
no distractions.
He was there for me, and I for him
to affirm our glory together.

Even though I have been awake,
my alarm clock crowed.
It is time to get up. It is 6:05 AM.
Once I was awakened.
He stayed with me, which was most of the night.

He leaves me this morning without fear or doubt,
but full of tears of joy, grounded in faith.
Still a mystery.
I never call him by his name,
but he's my Boo, my sweet.

I know he will be here again tonight
but will he wake me?
Tonight will be full moon - more fulfilling still,
celestial, ethereal!

Indescribable Pleasure

There is an indescribable burning, yearning
inside of me knowing there is something more
beyond unopened doors,
yet for me to unfold and to discover.

I'm always startled by the abundance of beauty
that surrounds me the majestic sprawling
canopies of forever green
and bearded oak trees

The daily kiss and flow
of the gliding sparkling scenic Hillsborough River
leaves me gasping for breath

it is sometimes sprinkled
with a blanket of fresh fallen young leaves
reflecting God's constant goodness
and His presence, His abounding power and mercy

I'm reminded of the ocean and
its roar ebb and splash billowing waves
white foam suggesting an appetite a sensation
undulating in a cadence and rhythm
so beguiling and captivating it beckons me shouts,
says my name stirs the fire in my soul
with an immersing and trembling pleasure

It ultimately consumes me, absorbs me
I am complete in its presence
it complements my beauty and
the mystery within me, if I am still, long enough
I lose myself all of my senses
and we become one

I wish the sun would melt me, smelt me
into the sugar-powdered sand when the tides rise
and the surf breaks it would engulf me, take me
pull me into a sweet forever dance with the sea
splashing me, thrusting me back forth,
up and down, loving me to freedom.

Reflections

Your Poem

*"She speaks with wisdom
and
faithful instruction
is on her tongue"*

Proverbs 31:26 NIV

"thus saith the Lord".

About The Author

The cover and this photograph embody my spirit, revealing who I was, who I am, and who I will always be.— Elizabeth P. Brooks

Elizabeth P. Brooks, the official poet laureate of the Rescuing History Authors Tour 2026, is a pioneer, poet, and reference librarian whose life's work is rooted in human dignity, social justice, and the transformative power of words. At the age of 20, she demonstrated remarkable courage and sacrifice by leaving her immediate family in Trinidad and Tobago to pursue the American Dream in New York City and create new opportunities for future generations. She later relocated to Los Angeles to raise her children, experiencing bicoastal living during pivotal periods of her life.

As an adult, Elizabeth returned to New York City to pursue higher education as a Lehman scholar in the Bronx, and Tanaka scholar Japan where she earned her undergraduate degree in

Sociology. She was soon hired by the New York Public Library and continued her academic journey at Pratt Institute in Brooklyn, earning her Master of Science in Library and Information Science (MS LIS). Her greatest joy has been serving diverse communities and empowering individuals through access to information.

In 2000, Elizabeth returned to California, where she led a team at La Pintoresca of the Pasadena Public Library. In recognition of her outstanding and invaluable service, she and her team received Certificates of Special Congressional Recognition from the office of Congressman Adam B. Schiff. She continued her service as a part-time reference librarian at Saint Leo University in Dade City. She move to Tampa and volunteered as an adult literacy tutor. Today she calls the Tampa Bay Area home and remains deeply committed to lifelong learning, and meaningful social change.

Elizabeth is the author of the powerful poetry chapbook *You May Applaud Now - Ed 2,* officially released on March 1, 2026, in celebration of Women's History Month. This compelling collection reflects her lived experiences, resilience, and distinctive voice as a performance poet.

She is also the author of *Unleashed,* a work that further affirms her commitment to truth-telling, creative expression, and personal liberation through literature. Her poems and nonfiction essays have been published in the Indiana Voice Journal, an online literary publication, where her writing continues to inspire and engage readers.

A member of Grace Family Church in Ybor City, Florida, Elizabeth is known for her outgoing spirit, her love of laughter, and her unwavering belief in the power of words to inspire, heal, and transform. She continues to write, perform, and develop new literary projects that reflect her enduring mission to uplift, educate, and empower others.